RACE WALKING AN ORIGIN STORY
AND OTHER MUSINGS

by Jeff Salvage

Copyright 2024, Salvage Writes Media
ISBN: 9798343571578
First Edition
Medford, NJ 08055

DEDICATION

This book is dedicated to Jennifer, my bride of over 16 years. We have been very fortunate to have traveled together to over 50 countries. On one of those trips, we walked over an ancient bridge in China, where legend has it that holding your breath while traversing it grants you two lifetimes together. I can't imagine anyone else I'd want to share not just one, but two lifetimes with. Whether it's training our new puppy or working on a simple house project, every day is an adventure.

Jennifer embodies what truly matters in life. Every day she is quietly helping those without a voice. She is kindhearted beyond words. She is equally supportive of my many crazy endeavors like this book and the video that inspired it. Whether it's as a sounding board for the initial concepts or providing feedback along the way, Jennifer continually elevates my efforts. These efforts, at least of late, rarely show a profit, but her encouragement for them is unwavering.

ACKNOWLEDGEMENTS

While not part of this book, I wanted to thank Brian Sanyshyn for his contributions to the video portions of this project. You can see some of his other work at *BrianSanyshynMusic.com*.

Additionally, many thanks go to Rob Lloyd whose generous time and expertise vastly improved the video which was the source material for the *Origin* story.

Last but not least, thanks to Gary Westerfield, a lifelong mentor whose tall tale at practice was the kernel that sprouted this yarn.

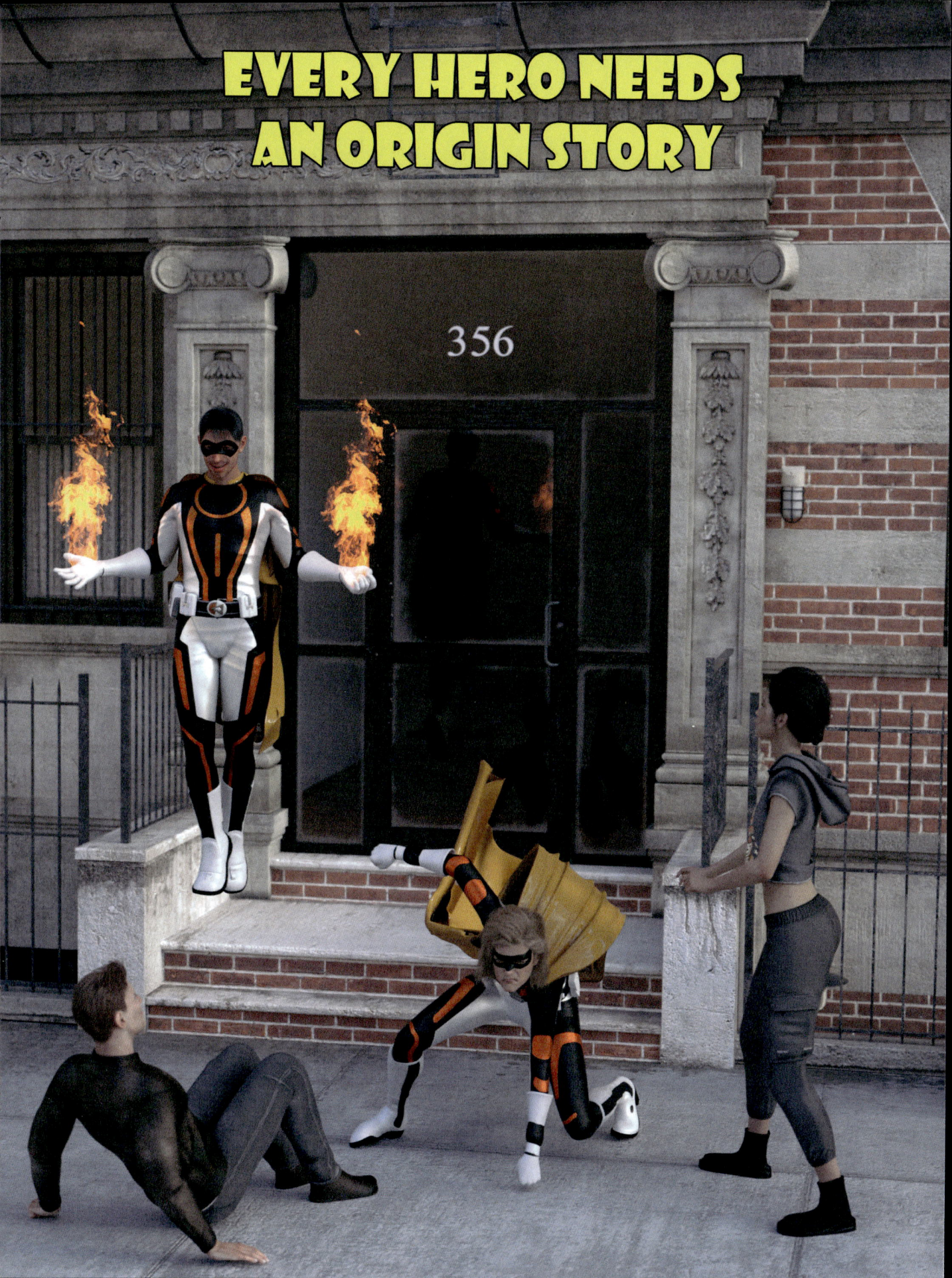

EVERY HERO NEEDS AN ORIGIN STORY

THE GREAT RACE WALKERS OF TODAY ARE NO DIFFERENT

MANY MOONS AGO

LONG BEFORE THE BIRTH OF MODERN ATHLETICS

THE WORLD WAS DEVOID OF RACE WALKERS

UNTIL AN OLD SHOEMAKER, PAPA CORDWAINER,

HAD A SON.

OSWALD GREW UP QUICKLY,

BUT MUCH TO HIS FATHER'S DISMAY, DID NOT WISH TO LEARN HIS FATHER'S CRAFT.

INSTEAD, OSWALD FOCUSED ON WINNING THE "WALK THE TOWN."

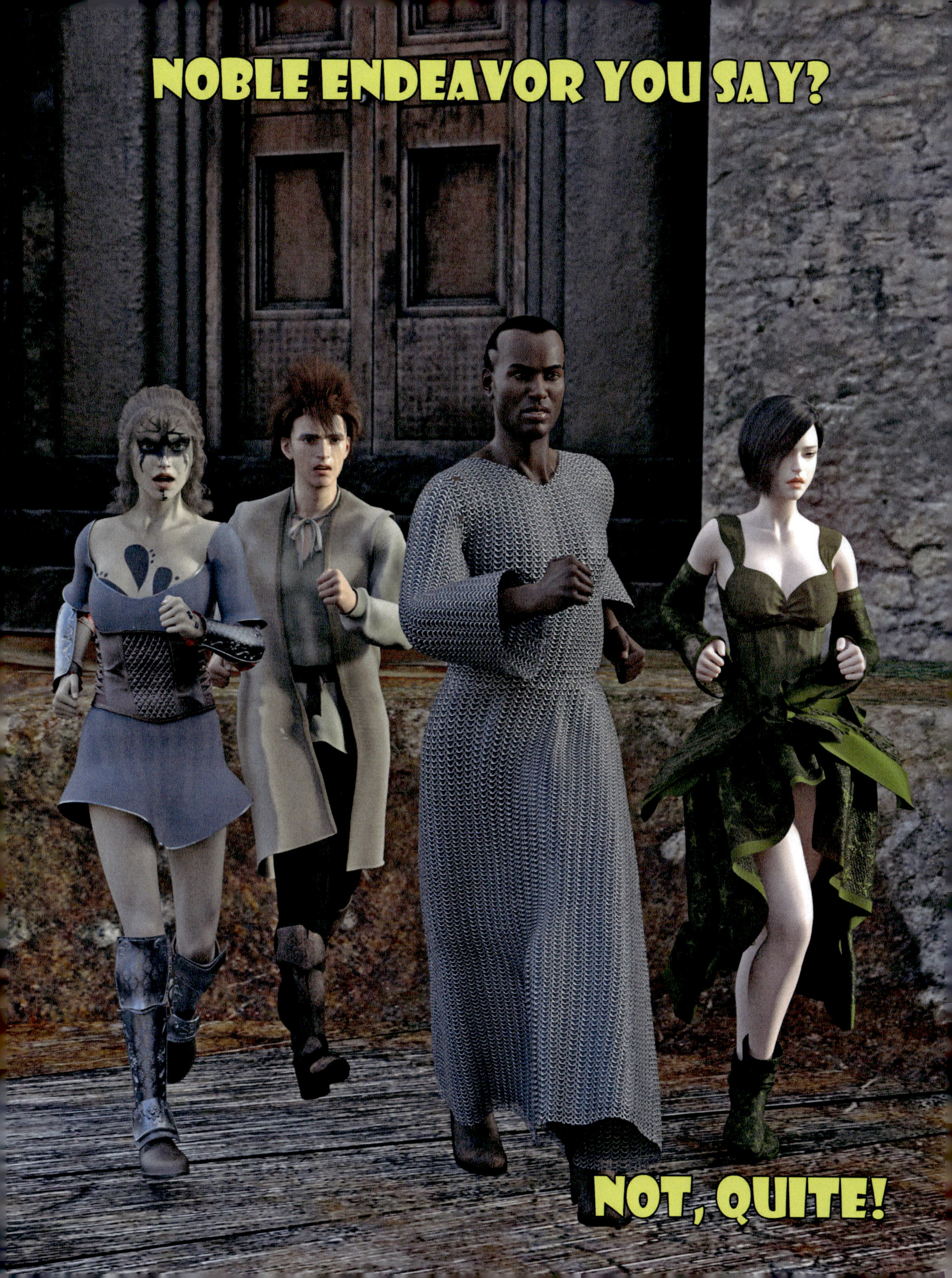
NOBLE ENDEAVOR YOU SAY?
NOT, QUITE!

WALKING THE TOWN IN MEDIEVAL TIMES WAS A RACE TO CROSS THE VILLAGE AS QUICKLY AS POSSIBLE,

BUT, WHILE DOWNING A DRINK IN EVERY TAVERN!

NOW, OSWALD WAS A BARFLY,

BUT ALAS WOULD LOSE YEAR AFTER YEAR TO FITTER FOLKS.

BEGRUDGINGLY, OSWALD ASKED FOR HIS DAD'S HELP.

HIS DAD TAUGHT HIM THE CURIOUS WIGGLE OF AGILE WALKERS.

HE EVEN CREATED AN AMAZING PAIR OF ATHLETIC SHOES.

OSWALD TRAINED HARD,

BUT ONLY ONCE THE TOWN WAS TUCKED AWAY IN A SLUMBER.

WHY YOU ASK? OSWALD WAS ASHAMED OF HIS HIP SWAY AND THUS WADDLED ONLY AT NIGHT.

WHEN THE COMPETITION FINALLY CAME, OSWALD COMBINED HIS DRINKING DEXTERITY WITH CHAMPIONSHIP WALKING FORM AND CRUSHED THE COMPETITION.

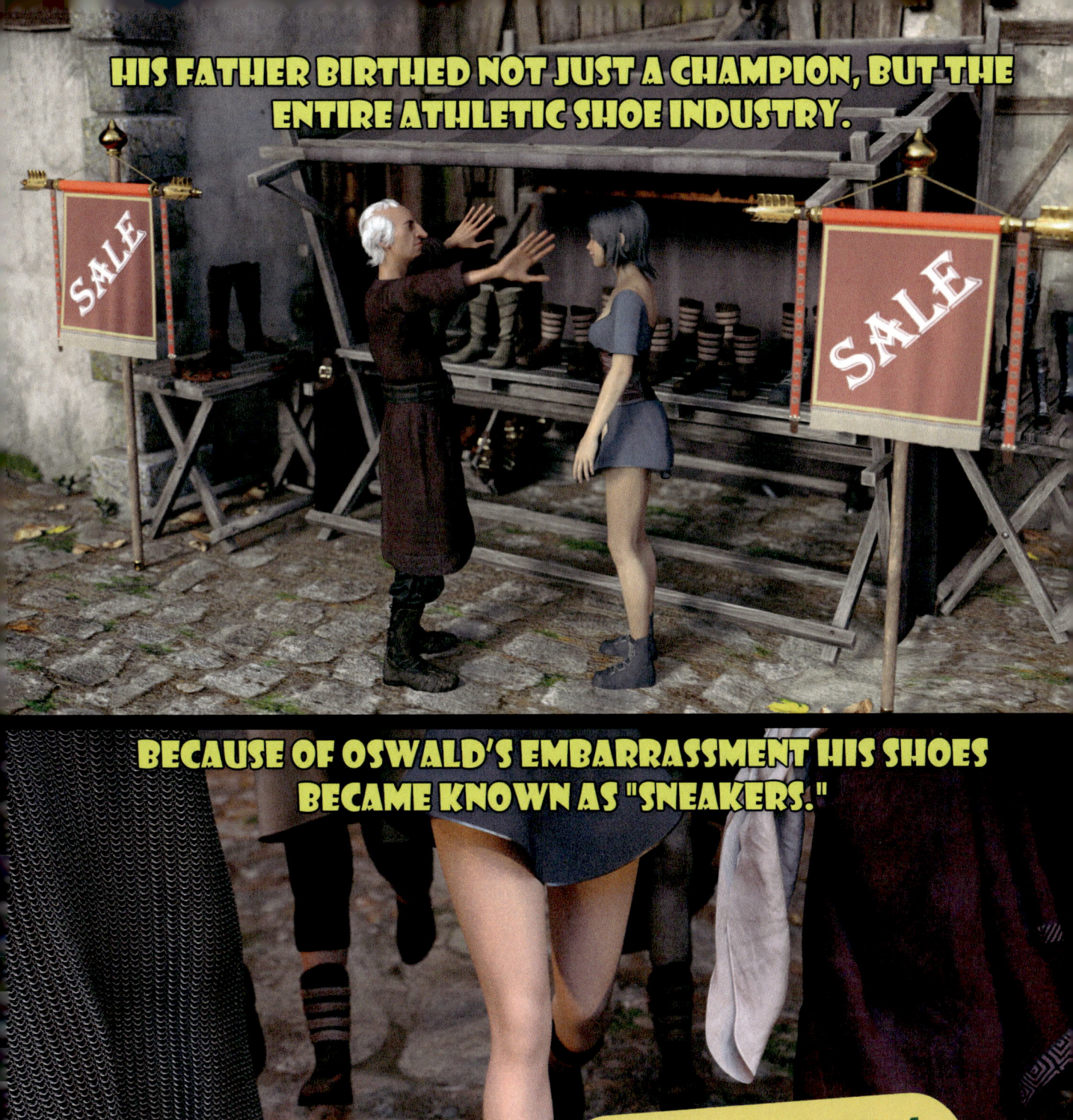

HIS FATHER BIRTHED NOT JUST A CHAMPION, BUT THE ENTIRE ATHLETIC SHOE INDUSTRY.

BECAUSE OF OSWALD'S EMBARRASSMENT HIS SHOES BECAME KNOWN AS "SNEAKERS."

BUY 2 GET 1 FREE

GOING OUT TRICK-OR-TREATING THIS HALLOWEEN?

BE CAREFUL WHICH HOUSES YOU APPROACH

AND IF YOU NEED TO GET AWAY IN A HURRY

LEARN TO RACE WALK & HAVE A HAPPIER HALLOWEEN!

PLANNING TO GORGE YOURSELF THIS THANKSGIVING?

PERHAPS YOU SHOULD TAKE UP THE LOW-IMPACT SPORT OF RACE WALKING!

WHO WILL SAVE CHRISTMAS WHEN THE REINDEER ARE TOO SICK TO FLY SANTA'S SLEIGH?

MRS. CLAUS AND THE ELVES?

NOPE, IT'S THE RACE WALKERS OF COURSE!

SOME SAY RACE WALKING ISN'T AS COOL AS SOME NEW OLYMPIC EVENTS

BUT WE KNOW RACE WALKING IS THE HIPPEST SPORT AROUND!

WHAT WOULD CAUSE A MERMAID TO GIVE UP HER FINS FOR FEET?

HER WISH TO JOIN HER FRIENDS AND RACE WALK!

COMING SOON!

Hobbits with Hip Action

ABOUT THE MUSINGS

This book evolved from a series of race walking animations I created over time. You can see more of them at

https://www.youtube.com/@Racewalk

Why create all of these animations in the first place? Because of the love I, and others, have for our event of race walking and our desire to spread the word of race walking to the masses. If you are reading this, clearly you also have a love for race walking and hopefully you would also like to help spread the word. What can you do?

Please visit *www.usaracewalking.org* and consider making a tax deductible donation to help with our mission in assisting college age and younger elite racewalkers in their quest for national and international prominence in racewalking.